Saying goodbye to...
A Grandparent

Chrysalis Education

Distributed in the United States by
Smart Apple Media
1980 Lookout Drive
North Mankato, Minnesota 56003

Copyright © Chrysalis Books PLC 2003

ISBN 1-93233-316-9

The Library of Congress control number 2003102443

Editorial manager: Joyce Bentley
Senior editor: Sarah Nunn
Project editor: Jean Coppendale
Designer: Clare Sleven
Illustrations by: Sarah Roper
Picture researcher: Jenny Barlow
Consultant: Jenni Thomas, Chief Executive
The Child Bereavement Trust

Printed in China

Foreword

Confronting death and dying as an adult is difficult, but addressing these issues with children is even harder. Children need to hear the truth and sharing a book can encourage and help both adults and children to talk openly and honestly about their feelings. This is something many of us find difficult to do.

Written in a clear, sensitive, and very caring way, the **Saying Goodbye To...** series will help parents, carers, and teachers to meet the needs of grieving children. Reading about the variety of real life situations, including the death of a pet, may enable children to feel less alone and more able to make sense of the bewildering emotions and responses they feel when someone dies.

Being alongside grieving children is not easy, the **Saying Goodbye To...** series will help make this challenging task a little less daunting.

Jenni Thomas OBE
Chief Executive
The Child Bereavement Trust

The Child Bereavement Trust
Registered Charity No. 04049

All reasonable efforts have been made to trace the relevant copyright holders of the images contained within this book. If we were unable to reach you, please contact Chrysalis Children's Books.

Cover Bubbles/Loisjoy Thurston 1 Bubbles/Clarissa Leahy 4 Bubbles/Loisjoy Thurston 5 Bubbles/Chris Rout 6 Corbis/Tom Stewart 7 Corbis/Mug Shots 8 Bubbles/Denise Hager 9 Bubbles/Loisjoy Thurston 10 Bubbles/Clarissa Leahy 11 Getty Images/David Harry Stewart 12 Bubbles/Jennie Woodcock 13 Bubbles/Chris Rout 14 Bubbles/Peter Sylent 15 Bubbles/Angela Hampton 16 Corbis/Nathan Benn 17 Getty Images/Jean Louis Batt 18 Bubbles/Loisjoy Thurston 19 Bubbles/Angela Hampton 20 Corbis/Jon Feingersh 21 Bubbles/Loisjoy Thurston 22 Corbis/David Turnley 23 Getty Images/Zigy Kaluzny 24 Corbis/Philip Gould 25 Photofusion/Paul Baldesere 26 Bubbles/Loisjoy Thurston 27 Bubbles/Angela Hampton 28 Bubbles/Peter Sylent 29 Corbis/Tom & Dee Ann McCarthy.

Contents

Growing old   4

What death means   6

Part of the family   8

Far away from home   10

A special relationship   12

It's not fair!   14

Feeling sad   16

Asking questions   18

Helping each other   20

Preparing for a funeral   22

Saying goodbye   24

Sharing memories   26

Part of your life   28

Glossary   30

Useful addresses   31

Index   32

Growing old

Children often feel very close to their grandparents. They can be an important part of their lives, and when they die children may feel terribly sad. Growing old is a natural part of life. People fall ill more often as they get older. Sometimes children visit and help grandparents who are unwell.

As people grow old, their bodies gradually wear out and stop working as well as they used to.

Something to think about...
At first, it might upset you to see someone you care about looking unwell. But old people who are ill usually find it **comforting** to see their grandchildren and like to spend time with them.

Rosa liked to help her grandma.

What death means

When someone dies, their body stops working and cannot be mended. Breathing stops, the heart stops beating, and the brain doesn't work any more. A dead person can't feel afraid or be in pain. It can be hard for children to believe that they won't see their grandparent again. This may make them feel very sad.

When Jake's grandma was dying, he visited her at the **hospice**. He was glad she was in a peaceful place with kind people to look after her.

Saying goodbye to a grandparent

Cara cried when her mom told her that her grandad had died.

Something to think about...
It's natural to want to ask lots of questions about what has happened when someone dies.

7

Part of the family

Some children see their grandparents often and get to know them well. Sometimes grandparents live in the same house as the rest of the family. If they become ill, the children may help to look after them. The old people may be ill for a long time.

Grandparents are an important part of many families.

Something to think about...
When someone dies after a long illness, it's natural to have lots of different feelings and even feel **relieved** that the person is not suffering any more.

Some grandparents help to look after their grandchildren while the parents are out at work.

Far away from home

Some children don't see their grandparents very much. Their grandparents may live too far away for them to visit very often. Perhaps they even live in a different country.

Jane and Matt's grandma taught them all about the different trees and flowers in her garden.

Children who don't know their grandparents well sometimes don't feel sad when they die. They may worry because they think they ought to feel sad. But there is no right or wrong way to feel when someone dies.

Henry loved spending time talking with his grandad. His grandad always had lots of stories to tell him.

A special relationship

Grandparents often like giving their grandchildren special treats, or taking them for days out. They may let their grandchildren do things that their parents wouldn't allow them to do. They may tell them off less, too! When the old people die, their grandchildren may feel very sad because they know how much they'll miss them.

Anya's grandparents loved taking her on trips to the seashore.

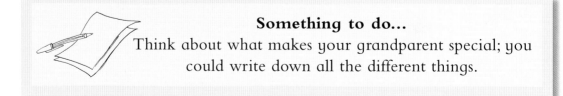

Something to do...
Think about what makes your grandparent special; you could write down all the different things.

12

Rosa felt that she could tell her grandma anything.

It's not fair!

Children who are **grieving** can have lots of confusing feelings when their grandparents die. They may think it's unfair that their friends' grandparents are still alive.

When Danny's grandma died, he was cross with his friend Alastair. He thought Alastair didn't understand how he was feeling.

They may be cross that life just carries on normally for everyone else. Some children may even feel angry with their grandparent for dying and leaving them to feel so sad. These are natural ways to feel when someone dies.

Gina was glad her grandmother had taught her how to draw. It would always remind Gina of grandma.

Something to think about...
If you are feeling angry because your grandparent has died, it can help if you share your feelings with someone you **trust**.

Feeling sad

Children can feel terribly sad and lost when their grandparent dies. They find it hard to understand that they will never see them again. Some children feel like crying when they are sad. Crying can be a good way of letting sad feelings out. But other children can feel just as sad without crying.

Mark cried when he thought about how much he missed his grandma.

Something to think about...
Sharing feelings of grief with other people can help everyone to comfort each other.

When Rachel's grandpa died, she could see
that her mom was very upset
because he had been her
daddy. Rachel was
worried about her
mom. She gave
her mom
a big hug.

Asking questions

When someone dies, it's natural for children to want to ask questions to help them understand what has happened. Sometimes adults try to **protect** children by not talking about what has happened. They worry that explaining things to children might upset them. Children may try to protect their parents, too. They may not ask questions in case it upsets their mom and dad. But being left out can just make children feel more confused and worried.

People told Tim his grandad had gone to "a better place." Tim didn't understand what they meant. He wondered whether it was a place he could visit.

Saying goodbye to a grandparent

Ling's dad helped her when her grandmother died by answering all her questions.

Something to think about...
If you are worried about anything, tell someone you trust about your feelings. They'll talk to you about your questions, even if they don't have all the answers.

19

Helping each other

When an old person dies, they may leave behind their husband or wife, their children, and their grandchildren. This means that many people can be left feeling sad and lonely. Families who are **mourning** can help each other during this very sad time. This could be by doing something practical, such as helping out with the shopping—or just by being around to listen when someone feels like talking.

David's dad gave him his grandfather's watch. It would always remind him of his grandad.

Something to do...
Think about what you could do to help a grandparent who has been **bereaved**. You could spend time with them, help with the garden, go for walks, or look at old family photographs together.

Lucy and her grandma talked together for a long time when Lucy's grandpa died. It helped both of them.

Preparing for a funeral

A **funeral** is a special service in which people come together to remember the person who has died. The dead body is brought to the funeral in a **coffin**. Some funerals are **religious**, others are not—because people have different beliefs. Children need to know what will happen at the funeral so that they can decide whether or not they would like to go to it.

Luke helped to choose the flowers for his grandma's funeral.

Saying goodbye to a grandparent

Sara chose a hymn
for the choir
to sing at her
grandad's funeral.

Something to think about...
If you decide not to go to your grandparent's funeral,
you could still take part by helping to get things
ready for it. You could help choose some flowers, or
write some special words or a prayer.

23

Saying goodbye

At a funeral, people who cared about the person who has died show their **respect** for them and say goodbye. It can be difficult for children to see the people they love looking upset and crying. But it's natural to feel sad at a funeral and people are there to comfort each other.

Laura sat with her mom at her grandpa's funeral service. She was pleased to be there with her family to say goodbye.

Saying goodbye to a grandparent

A funeral gives people a chance to share their memories of the person who has died.

Something to do...
You might decide to take part in the funeral in some way. For example, you could help people to find their seats or you could light a candle. It's up to you.

Sharing memories

When an old person dies, lots of people in the family are affected by their death and have their own memories to share. Families may feel particularly sad on special days, such as at Christmas, **Diwali**, or **Hanukah**.

Looking at photos helped Jade to remember the happy times she'd spent with her grandma.

At these times, there may be lots of reminders that the person isn't around any more. But people can talk about the person who died and remember some of the things that they did together.

Fiona helped to look after her grandad's special plants.

Something to do...
Think about what you could do to help you remember your grandparent. All your memories are like gifts you will always have from your grandparent.

Part of your life

It can take time to feel happy again after someone you love has died. Grieving is natural and you can't hurry it. After a while, your memories of the person who died will not feel as sad. It can also help children when they think that their grandparent was able to enjoy a long life.

Jonathan was glad he'd known his grandad. He felt lucky because he knew that not all children have the chance to know their grandparents.

Something to think about...
Sharing memories can help people to comfort each other and feel happier during sad times. It's natural to feel both happy and sad when you're grieving.

Nina's family often used her grandma's favorite pot at meal times. It helped everyone to remember her.

Glossary

bereaved	being left behind when someone you love or care about dies
coffin	the container in which a dead body is placed
comforting	helping someone who is sad to feel better
Diwali	an important festival in the Hindu religion
funeral	a special service in which people remember a person who has died and say goodbye to them
grieving	the natural process of feeling sad after someone has died
guilty	feeling bad, as if it's your fault that something is wrong
Hanukah	the Jewish festival of light
hospice	a building where people who are dying are looked after
mourning	the ways in which people who have been bereaved show their feelings of grief
mosque	a holy building where Muslims worship
protect	taking care of someone, keeping them from harm
relief	to feel happier after a difficult time
religious	to do with a belief in God
respect	a polite attitude or manner which shows that someone is thought well of
trust	feeling that someone will not let you down

Useful addresses

The Bereavement Journey
Anyone who has lost a loved one is welcome to contact this organization.
535 Mountain Ave
Winnipeg, Manitoba
R2W 1K8
Website: www. thebereavementjourney.com

The Compassionate Friends, Inc
An organization offering grief support and written information.
P.O. Box 369
Oak Brock, IL
60522-3696
Toll-free tel: 877-969-0010
Website: www.compassionatefriends.org

Grief and loss.org
This support organization was started after the September 11, 2001 tragedy. Free help is offered to anyone suffering traumatic loss.
Toll-free tel: 1-866-797-2277
Website: www.griefandloss.org

Griefnet.org
An internet community dealing with death, grief, and loss—operated by the non-profit Rivendall Resources. The website includes KIDSAID, a safe environment for kids to ask questions and find information. Under the direction of a Michigan grief psychologist, KIDSAID has questions and answers, games, art, stories, poetry.
Website: www.rivendall.org/

Medlineplus health information
This service of the U.S. Library of Medicine has details of many publications, such as *Helping Young People with Death and Funerals*,

How to Help Your Child Deal with Death, *Talking to Children about Grief*.
Website: www.nlm.nih.gov.medlineplus/ bereavement.html

The National Center for Grieving Children and Their Families
The Dougy Center is the first U.S. center to offer peer support groups for grieving children. Over 13,500 children have been helped since 1982. Guide books available for children, and for adults helping children. Their website includes a list of organizations, many with local chapters offering support services.
Website: www.dougy.org

The Samaritans of Boston
654 Beacon St
6th Floor
Boston, MA
02215
A 24-hour befriending line for people in distress is manned by trained volunteers.
Tel: 617-247-0220

San Francisco Growth House Inc.
This organization offers information and resources related to grief and bereavement, including an online bookshop. Publications for helping children include *How Do We Tell the Children?*, *Mourning Children, Children Mourning*, *Helping Children Cope with the Loss of a Loved One*.
Website: www.growthhouse.org

www.bereavement.com is a sympathy sharing site open to all. There are articles and information resources at **www.bereavementmag.com**

31

Index

A
addresses 31
anger 15

B
bereaved 21, 30
Bereavement Journey 31

C
Christmas 26
coffin 22, 30
comfort 5, 16, 24, 29, 30
Compassionate Friends, Inc 31
confused feelings 14, 18
crying 7, 16, 24

D
death 6–7
Diwali 26, 30

F
family 8–9, 20–1, 24, 26
funeral 22–5, 30

G
grandparent, helping 21, 27
grieving 14, 16, 28–9, 30
growing old 4–5
guilt 30

H
Hanukah 26, 30
happy feelings 28
helping each other 20–1
hospice 6, 30

I
illness 4–5, 8

M
Medlineplus health information 31
memories 25, 26–7, 28, 29
missing grandparents 12, 16
mourning 20, 30

N
National Center for Grieving Children and Their Families 31

O
old age 4–5

P
parents 17, 18
photographs 21, 26
protecting children 18, 30

Q
questions 7, 18–19

R
relationship 12–13
relief 8, 30
religion 22, 30
respect 24, 30

S
sadness 6, 11, 12, 15, 16–17, 28

Samaritans of Boston 31
San Francisco Growth House Inc 31
saying goodbye 24–5
sharing feelings 16, 25

T
talking 13, 20, 21
treats 12
trust 15, 19, 30

V
visiting grandparents 10

W
worrying 11, 18–19
writing down feelings 12